Table of Contents

Appendix

Chapter 1: Introduction to AV CAD & Drafting Basics

What is AV CAD?

AV CAD (Audio-Visual Computer-Aided Design) involves the use of AutoCAD to create technical drawings and layouts for AV systems. These systems include:

- Conference rooms
- Theaters
- Stadiums
- Classrooms
- Smart homes

Why is AV CAD Important?

- Ensures accurate placement of AV equipment
- Helps integrators and contractors understand project requirements
- Standardizes AV design documentation
- Reduces errors and rework by providing clear blueprints

AutoCAD's Role in AV Design

AutoCAD allows AV designers to create precise layouts, wiring diagrams, and equipment placement plans for projects.

AutoCAD Interface Overview

- **Menu Bar & Ribbon** – Essential tools and commands
- **Command Line** – For entering commands and shortcuts
- **Toolbars & Panels** – Quick access to drawing tools
- **Model Space** – Area for actual drawing
- **Layout Tabs (Paper Space)** – For printing and setting up sheets
- **Properties Panel** – For modifying objects and viewing attributes
- **Status Bar** – Quick toggles for AutoCAD functions

Basic AutoCAD Navigation

- **Zoom In/Out: Scroll the mouse wheel**
- **Pan: Hold the mouse wheel and drag**
- **Undo/Redo: Use CTRL + Z and CTRL + Y**

Setting Up an AV Drawing

Step 1: Create a New Drawing

- **Open AutoCAD**
- **Click New Drawing**
- **Select a standard template (e.g., acad.dwt)**
- **Save the file as AV_Project_01.dwg**

Step 2: Configure Drawing Units

- **Type UNITS and press Enter**
- **Set:**
    - **Length: Decimal (or Architectural)**
    - **Precision: 0.00**
    - **Insertion Scale: Inches or Millimeters (depending on project requirements)**
- **Click OK**

Step 3: Set Up Layers

- **Type LAYER and press Enter**
- **Create the following layers:**
    - **AV_Devices (Color: Blue)**
    - **AV_Wiring (Color: Red)**
    - **Text_Labels (Color: Black)**
- **Click OK**

Hands-on Exercise

Objective: Create a basic AV layout with a title block.

Steps:

1. **Create a title block with the text "AV Design – Module 1"**

2. **Draw a basic AV layout:**

   o **Place a TV display (rectangle with label "TV")**

   o **Add two speakers (circles with label "Speaker")**

   o **Connect them using AV wiring (lines from the TV to the speakers)**

3. **Save the drawing as AV_Exercise_01.dwg**

Quiz

1. **What is the main function of AutoCAD in AV design?**

2. **What command do you use to set drawing units?**

3. **Name three essential AutoCAD interface components.**

4. **What is the shortcut command to draw a line in AutoCAD?**

5. **Why are layers important in AutoCAD?**

Conclusion & Next Steps

- **Practice creating simple AV layouts in AutoCAD**

- **Review industry standards for AV documentation**

- **Get ready for Chapter 2: AutoCAD Essentials for AV Design**

Chapter 2: AutoCAD Essentials for AV Design

Creating a New AutoCAD File

- **Open AutoCAD and click New Drawing**
- **Choose a template (acad.dwt or custom AV template)**
- **Save the file as AV_Project_02.dwg**

Configuring Drawing Units

- **Type UNITS and press Enter**
- **Set:**
  - **Length Type: Decimal or Architectural**
  - **Precision: 0.00 or appropriate for the project**
  - **Insertion Scale: Inches or Millimeters**
- **Click OK**

Understanding the Drawing Limits and Grid

- **Type LIMITS and define a working area**
- **Enable the grid using F7**

Working with Layers in AutoCAD

What Are Layers?

Layers help organize different AV components and improve drawing clarity.

Creating Layers for AV Design

- **Type LAYER and press Enter**
- **Create the following layers:**
  - **AV_Devices (Color: Blue)**
  - **AV_Wiring (Color: Red)**
  - **Text_Labels (Color: Black)**
  - **Dimensions (Color: Green)**
- **Assign appropriate line types to each layer**
- **Click OK to apply changes**

Essential AutoCAD Commands for AV Design

Basic Drawing Commands

- **L – Line**
- **C – Circle**
- **REC – Rectangle**
- **PL – Polyline**

Editing Commands

- **TR – Trim**
- **EX – Extend**
- **COPY – Duplicates objects**
- **MOVE – Moves objects**
- **ROTATE – Rotates objects**

Annotation Commands

- **TEXT – Adds single-line text**
- **MTEXT – Adds multi-line text**
- **DIM – Creates dimensions**
- **LEADER – Adds callout annotations**

Hands-on Exercise

Objective: Create an AV drawing with basic elements.

Steps:

1. **Set up a new drawing with units and limits**
2. **Create layers for AV design**
3. **Draw a basic AV system layout:**
   - **Insert a TV display (rectangle with label "TV")**
   - **Place four speakers (circles labeled "Speaker")**
   - **Connect them using AV wiring (red polylines)**
   - **Annotate the drawing with labels and dimensions**
4. **Save the file as AV_Exercise_02.dwg**

Chapter 3: AV Symbols, Blocks & Standards

Understanding AV Symbols

What Are AV Symbols?

AV symbols are standardized representations of AV equipment in technical drawings. These symbols ensure that all professional installers, engineers, and clients can interpret designs easily and accurately.

Common AV Symbols and Their Uses

- **Displays (TVs, projectors, monitors)** – Typically represented as rectangles with diagonal lines

- **Speakers** – Shown as circles with soundwave indicators

- **Microphones** – Represented as small circles with stems

- **AV Racks** – Depicted as rectangles with U-space markings

- **Cabling & Signal Paths** – Drawn as different line styles based on signal type

Industry Standards for AV Symbols

Adhering to AV industry standards ensures consistency across all projects. The following organizations provide guidelines for AV drafting and design:

- **AVIXA (Audiovisual and Integrated Experience Association)** – Defines industry best practices for AV system design

- **BICSI (Building Industry Consulting Service International)** – Sets structured cabling standards

- **ISO & ANSI Standards** – Provide global standardization for AV symbols and technical drawings

- **ADA Compliance** – Ensures accessibility considerations in AV placement

Using Blocks in AutoCAD for AV Design

What Are AutoCAD Blocks?

Blocks are reusable objects in AutoCAD that simplify drafting by allowing you to insert pre-defined AV symbols.

Creating Blocks for AV Symbols

1. Draw the symbol using basic AutoCAD tools (Line, Circle, Polyline, etc.).
2. Type BLOCK and press Enter to open the Block Definition dialog.
3. Assign a name (e.g., "AV_Speaker" or "AV_Display").
4. Select objects to include in the block.
5. Specify an insertion point (the point where the block will be placed).
6. Click OK to save the block for future use.

Inserting Blocks in AV Drawings

- Use INSERT to place pre-created blocks into your drawing.
- Use DYNAMIC BLOCKS to create adjustable AV symbols (e.g., scalable projectors).

Hands-on Exercise

Objective: Create a custom AutoCAD block for an AV speaker.

Steps:

1. Draw a speaker symbol (a circle with a soundwave).
2. Convert it into a block (BLOCK command).
3. Save and insert it into an AV layout (INSERT command).
4. Label the speaker and connect it using signal paths.
5. Save the drawing as AV_Exercise_03.dwg.

Quiz

1. What is the purpose of using AV symbols in AutoCAD?
2. What command is used to create a block in AutoCAD?
3. Name three common AV symbols.
4. Why are industry standards important for AV design?
5. What is the benefit of using dynamic blocks in AutoCAD?

Conclusion & Next Steps

✓ Standardize AV symbols in your design workflow.
✓ Utilize blocks for efficient drafting.
✓ Get ready for Chapter 4: Signal Flow Diagrams & Line Types.

Chapter 4: Signal Flow Diagrams & Line Types

Understanding AV Signal Flow

What is a Signal Flow Diagram?

A signal flow diagram represents the path of audio, video, and control signals between AV components. It ensures proper connectivity and aids in troubleshooting.

Key Components in a Signal Flow Diagram

- **Sources** (Laptops, Media Players, Microphones)
- **Processors** (Mixers, DSPs, AV Switchers)
- **Outputs** (Speakers, Displays, Projectors)
- **Cabling & Connectors** (HDMI, XLR, Ethernet, Fiber)

Line Types for AV Signal Flow

Standard Line Types and Their Meanings

- **Solid Line**: Video signal (HDMI, SDI, VGA)
- **Dashed Line**: Audio signal (Balanced, Unbalanced, Mic Level)
- **Dotted Line**: Control signal (RS-232, TCP/IP, IR)
- **Bold Line**: Power connections

Creating and Managing Line Types in AutoCAD

1. Open **Layer Manager (LAYER command)**.
2. Create new layers for **Video, Audio, Control, and Power**.
3. Assign different line types to each layer.
4. Adjust **line weights** for clear visibility.

Drawing a Signal Flow Diagram in AutoCAD

Step-by-Step Process

1. Define system components (**Sources, Processors, Outputs**).
2. Draw symbols for each device.
3. Connect components using the correct **line types**.
4. Label each signal path with **its type and direction**.
5. Organize the layout for **easy interpretation**.

Hands-on Exercise

Objective: Create a simple AV signal flow diagram for a conference room.

Steps:

1. Place **source devices** (Laptop, Blu-ray player) on the left.

2. Add a **processor** (AV switcher) in the center.

3. Place **output devices** (Projector, speakers) on the right.

4. Connect devices using **proper line types and labels**.

5. Save the drawing as **AV_Exercise_04.dwg**.

Quiz

1. What is the purpose of a signal flow diagram?

2. Which line type represents audio signals in AutoCAD?

3. How do you assign a specific line type to a layer?

4. What are common AV signal types found in a system?

5. Why is it important to label signal paths?

Conclusion & Next Steps

✅ Practice drawing different **signal flow scenarios**.

✅ Standardize **line types and layers** for consistency.

✅ Prepare for Chapter 5: **Rack Elevations & Equipment Layouts**.

Chapter 5: Rack Elevations & Equipment Layouts

Understanding AV Rack Layouts

What is an AV Rack?

An AV rack is a standardized enclosure that houses AV equipment, ensuring **organization, accessibility, and proper ventilation**.

Types of AV Racks

- **Floor-Standing Racks**: Common for **large-scale installations**.
- **Wall-Mounted Racks**: Suitable for **smaller rooms or network closets**.
- **Slide-Out & Rotating Racks**: Used in **high-maintenance environments** for easy access.

Key Considerations for Rack Design

- **Weight Distribution**: Place heavier components at the bottom.
- **Cooling & Ventilation**: Ensure airflow for heat dissipation.
- **Accessibility**: Design for easy maintenance and cable management.
- **Cable Management**: Use Velcro ties, raceways, and lacing bars.

Rack Elevations & Equipment Placement

Standard Rack Units (U-Space)

- **1U = 1.75 inches** in height.
- Standard racks are **42U, 27U, 14U, or 9U**.

Best Practices for Equipment Placement

- **Power Distribution Units (PDU)** at the top or bottom.
- **AV Switchers, DSPs, and Servers** in the middle for better weight distribution.
- **Amplifiers** at the bottom to maintain stability.
- **Ventilation and Cooling Fans** for heat management.
- **Patch Panels & Cable Management Units** placed strategically for organized wiring.

Creating a Rack Elevation in AutoCAD

1. Set up a **vertical layout** using correct **U-space measurements**.
2. Draw **rectangles representing equipment** with accurate dimensions.
3. Label each device with **model numbers and descriptions**.
4. Use **layers to distinguish power, audio, and video components**.
5. Incorporate **annotations for easy identification** of rack components.

Hands-on Exercise

Objective: Design a **42U AV rack layout** for a control room.

Steps:

1. Create a **rack outline** using **standard U-spacing**.
2. Add essential components (**PDU, DSP, amplifier, switcher, server**).
3. Label each device with **annotations**.
4. Organize **cabling paths** for **power and signal separation**.
5. Include **ventilation and access considerations**.
6. Save the drawing as **AV_Exercise_05.dwg**.

Quiz

1. What is the height of **1U** in rack space?
2. Why should **amplifiers** be placed at the bottom of a rack?
3. What AutoCAD command is useful for **labeling devices**?
4. Why is **cable management** crucial in rack design?
5. What **layer management technique** helps distinguish different signals in a rack layout?

Conclusion & Next Steps

✓ Refine **rack layout designs** based on **industry best practices**.

✓ Experiment with **different equipment configurations**.

✓ Standardize **cabling and labeling methods**.

✓ Prepare for Chapter 6: **Floor Plans & AV System Integration**.

Chapter 6: Floor Plans & AV System Integration

Understanding Floor Plans for AV Design

What is a Floor Plan?

A floor plan is a scaled diagram of a room or building viewed from above. It shows spatial relationships, structural elements, and AV device placements.

Essential Elements of an AV Floor Plan

- **Room Layout**: Walls, doors, windows, and furniture
- **AV Devices**: Projectors, speakers, microphones, control panels
- **Cabling Paths**: Routes for power and signal cables
- **Electrical & Network Outlets**: Integration with building infrastructure

Placing AV Devices in Floor Plans

Best Practices for Device Placement

- **Displays & Projectors**: Ensure clear sightlines and correct throw distances
- **Speakers**: Position for even sound distribution
- **Microphones**: Avoid feedback and ensure optimal pickup
- **Control Panels**: Place within user reach for accessibility

Using AutoCAD to Insert AV Components

1. Set up a **floor plan as an external reference (XREF)**.
2. Use **blocks for AV symbols** (TVs, speakers, microphones).
3. Assign devices to **specific layers** (AV_Devices, AV_Wiring).
4. Annotate with **callouts and dimensions**.

Coordinating with Other Trades

Collaboration with Architects & Engineers

- **Electrical Coordination**: Ensure adequate power outlets for AV equipment.
- **HVAC Considerations**: Avoid placing AV devices near air vents.
- **Structural Adjustments**: Ensure proper mounting for heavy displays and speakers.

Common AV Integration Challenges

- **Cable Path Conflicts**: Routing through walls and ceilings.

- **Interference Issues**: Avoiding electrical noise in AV signals.

- **Space Constraints**: Ensuring sufficient room for equipment racks.

Hands-on Exercise

Objective: Design an AV system layout for a **conference room**.

Steps:

1. Import a **floor plan as an XREF**.

2. Place **AV devices** (displays, microphones, speakers) using blocks.

3. Draw **cabling routes** ensuring proper separation of **power and signal**.

4. Add **labels and dimensions** for clear documentation.

5. Save the drawing as **AV_Exercise_06.dwg**.

Quiz

1. What is the purpose of a floor plan in AV design?

2. Why is it important to coordinate AV placements with other trades?

3. What AutoCAD command is used to attach an external reference?

4. What layer types are essential for an AV floor plan?

5. Why is it important to consider HVAC placement in AV system integration?

✅ Develop proficiency in reading and modifying **architectural floor plans**.

✅ Improve **coordination with electrical and structural engineers**.

✅ Prepare for Chapter 7: **AutoCAD Annotations & Documentation**.

Chapter 7: AutoCAD Annotations & Documentation

Introduction to AutoCAD Annotations

What are Annotations?

Annotations provide **text-based information** in a drawing, making it easier to understand layouts, devices, and connections.

Types of Annotations in AutoCAD

- **Text Annotations** (Single-line text, Multi-line text)
- **Leaders & Callouts** (Used to point out specific objects)
- **Dimensions** (Linear, Aligned, Angular, Radial, and Diameter)
- **Tables & Schedules** (Used for equipment lists and specifications)

Adding Text & Callouts in AutoCAD

Creating Text Annotations

1. Use TEXT for **single-line text** or MTEXT for **multi-line text**.
2. Place text on **appropriate layers** (AV_Annotations).
3. Set **text height** based on drawing scale.
4. Use **standardized fonts** for consistency.

Using Leaders & Callouts

1. Use LEADER to create a **pointer annotation**.
2. Attach leaders to **AV devices** (e.g., projectors, speakers, displays).
3. Add descriptive **labels** (e.g., "HDMI Connection" or "Wall-Mounted Display").

Applying Dimensions in AutoCAD

Types of Dimensions & Their Uses

- **Linear Dimensions**: Measure straight-line distances.
- **Aligned Dimensions**: Follow the angle of an object.
- **Angular Dimensions**: Measure angles between two lines.
- **Radial & Diameter Dimensions**: Used for circular objects.

Adding Dimensions in AutoCAD

1. Use DIMLINEAR to **add linear dimensions**.

2. Use DIMALIGNED for **dimensions along a slanted object**.

3. Adjust **dimension styles (DIMSTYLE)** to ensure readability.

4. Place dimensions on an **annotation layer** (AV_Dimensions).

Hands-on Exercise

Objective: Annotate an AV system layout with **dimensions, labels, and an equipment schedule**.

Steps:

1. Insert **text labels** for all AV components.

2. Add **dimensions** to key locations.

3. Use **leaders and callouts** to indicate connections.

4. Create a **table listing all AV equipment** used in the layout.

5. Save the drawing as **AV_Exercise_07.dwg**.

Quiz

1. What command is used to add single-line text in AutoCAD?

2. How do leaders improve drawing annotations?

3. What is the difference between DIMLINEAR and DIMALIGNED?

4. Why is it important to use an equipment schedule?

5. What command creates a structured table in AutoCAD?

Conclusion & Next Steps

✅ Standardize **annotation styles** in all AV drawings.

✅ Improve clarity by using **leaders, tables, and dimensions**.

✅ Prepare for Chapter 8: **Future Trends in AV System Design.**

Chapter 8: Future Trends in AV System Design

Emerging Technologies in AV CAD

Integration of AI & Machine Learning in AutoCAD

- AI-based layout optimization for AV systems.
- Automated clash detection using AI-powered analysis.
- Predictive maintenance models for AV system longevity.

Building Information Modeling (BIM) for AV Integration

- Revit & BIM collaboration for better AV coordination.
- 3D modeling for accurate space planning.
- BIM-driven AV documentation and workflow automation.

Virtual & Augmented Reality in AV System Design

- VR simulations for pre-installation testing.
- AR overlays to assist with AV equipment placement.
- Real-time collaboration using cloud-based VR tools.

Sustainability & Energy-Efficient AV Systems

- Smart power management in AV rack design.
- Use of low-power AV devices to reduce energy consumption.
- Integration of renewable energy sources for AV installations.

Hands-on Exercise

Objective: Create a conceptual AV layout using BIM integration and AI tools.

Steps:

1. Open Revit or AutoCAD with BIM plugins.
2. Import an AV layout into a BIM environment.
3. Use AI-based tools to optimize layout efficiency.
4. Save the drawing as AV_FutureTrends_14.dwg.

Quiz

1. How does AI improve AV system design?

2. What are the benefits of integrating BIM into AV CAD workflows?

3. How can VR be used in AV design and installation?

4. What are some sustainable practices for AV system efficiency?

5. How does AI-powered clash detection improve AV installations?

Conclusion & Next Steps

✓ Stay updated on future AV CAD trends.

✓ Experiment with BIM, AI, and VR tools for AV system integration.

✓ Continue professional development in advanced AV CAD technologies.

✓ Prepare for Chapter 9: Display & Touch Panel Elevations in AV Design.

Chapter 9: Display & Touch Panel Elevations in AV Design

Understanding Display Elevations

What Are Display Elevations?

Display elevations provide **front and side views** of mounted displays, ensuring proper placement, viewing angles, and accessibility.

Types of Displays in AV Systems

- **Flat Panel Displays** (LCD, LED, OLED) – Used in **conference rooms, signage, classrooms**

- **Interactive Touch Panels** – Used for **meeting room control and digital signage**

- **Projection Screens** – Wall-mounted, retractable, or ceiling-recessed screens

Key Considerations for Display Placement

- **Viewing Angle & Sightlines**: Avoid obstructions and optimize visibility.

- **Mounting Height**: Consider ADA compliance and ergonomic positioning.

- **Power & Data Connectivity**: Ensure proper placement of outlets and cable routes.

Creating Display Elevation Drawings in AutoCAD

Best Practices for Display Elevation Drawings

- Use **orthographic views** (front, side, and top) for accuracy.

- Place displays on appropriate **layers** (AV_Displays, AV_Mounts).

- Annotate with **mounting details, dimensions, and labels**.

Step-by-Step Guide to Drawing Display Elevations

1. Create a new layer named AV_Displays.

2. Draw the display using a **rectangle**, ensuring accurate dimensions.

3. Add **mounting brackets** and label their attachment points.

4. Include **power and data outlets** in the elevation.

5. Use **leaders and callouts** for annotation (e.g., model, mounting height).

6. Save the drawing as **Display_Elevation_09.dwg**.

Hands-on Exercise

Objective: Create an elevation drawing for a **wall-mounted display with a touch panel**.

Steps:

1. Draw a **75-inch flat panel display** on a conference room wall.

2. Add a **touch panel** mounted near the conference table.

3. Include **dimensions and labels** for height, width, and mounting position.

4. Annotate connection points for **power and data**.

5. Save the file as **AV_Exercise_09.dwg**.

Quiz

1. What is the purpose of an elevation drawing in AV design?

2. What are the recommended mounting heights for touch panels?

3. How do you label a display's power and data outlets in AutoCAD?

4. What AutoCAD command is used to create a leader annotation?

5. Why is sightline analysis important in display placement?

✓ Improve **elevation detailing** for display integration.

✓ Coordinate **display placements** with electrical and interior design teams.

✓ Prepare for Chapter 10: **Ceiling Equipment Elevations in AV Design**.

Chapter 10: Ceiling Equipment Elevations in AV Design

Understanding Ceiling Equipment Elevations

What Are Ceiling Equipment Elevations?

Ceiling equipment elevations provide a **detailed layout** of AV devices mounted in or on the ceiling, ensuring proper positioning for **audio, video, and control functionality**.

Types of Ceiling Equipment in AV Systems

- **Projectors** – Ceiling-mounted for **large displays and presentations**.
- **Ceiling Speakers** – Used for **distributed audio in meeting rooms and auditoriums**.
- **Ceiling Microphones** – For **hands-free audio capture in conferencing spaces**.
- **Lighting & Sensors** – Integrated with AV systems for **automation and control**.

Key Considerations for Ceiling Equipment Placement

- **Projection Distance & Alignment**: Ensure correct **throw distance and screen positioning**.
- **Speaker Coverage & Distribution**: Optimize **placement for uniform sound dispersion**.
- **Microphone Pickup Zones**: Avoid **interference and ensure clear audio**.
- **Cable Routing & Power Access**: Plan for **clean installation and easy maintenance**.

Creating Ceiling Equipment Elevation Drawings in AutoCAD

Best Practices for Ceiling Elevation Drawings

- Use **top-down and section views** for clarity.
- Assign equipment to **appropriate layers** (AV_Projectors, AV_Speakers).
- Include **mounting details, dimensions, and annotations**.

Step-by-Step Guide to Drawing Ceiling Elevations

1. Create a new layer named AV_Ceiling_Devices.
2. Draw the **ceiling grid** and indicate **structural elements**.
3. Place **AV devices** (projectors, speakers, microphones) at specified locations.
4. Include **suspension/mounting brackets** where applicable.
5. Add **labels and annotations** for **model numbers and mounting heights**.
6. Save the drawing as **Ceiling_Elevation_10.dwg**.

Hands-on Exercise

Objective: Create a ceiling elevation drawing for an **auditorium AV setup**.

Steps:

1. Draw the **ceiling structure** with a **scaled grid**.
2. Position **ceiling-mounted projectors** with **throw distances**.
3. Add **distributed ceiling speakers** for **even sound coverage**.
4. Include **ceiling microphones** for **hands-free conferencing**.
5. Annotate connection points for **power and data**.
6. Save the file as **AV_Exercise_10.dwg**.

Quiz

1. What is the purpose of ceiling equipment elevation in AV design?
2. What are the recommended placement guidelines for ceiling speakers?
3. How do you label a projector's mounting bracket in AutoCAD?
4. Why is microphone pickup zone planning important in ceiling installations?
5. What AutoCAD command is used to create section views of ceiling layouts?

✓ Improve precision in **ceiling-mounted AV equipment layouts**.

✓ Coordinate **ceiling placements** with structural and electrical teams.

✓ Prepare for Chapter 11: **Essential AV Standards & AutoCAD Resources**.

Chapter 11: Essential AV Standards & AutoCAD Resources

Understanding AV Industry Standards

Key AV Industry Standards

- **AVIXA (Audiovisual and Integrated Experience Association)**
- **BICSI (Building Industry Consulting Service International)**
- **ISO & ANSI Standards** (International audiovisual guidelines)
- **ADA Compliance** for accessible design

Finding Equipment Specifications & AutoCAD Libraries

- Manufacturer websites: **Crestron, Extron, AMX, Shure, Biamp**
- Open-source AV symbol libraries: **AVIXA Resource Hub, DraftSight AV Symbols**

Hands-on Exercise

Objective: Research AVIXA standards and download a CAD block for an AV device.

Conclusion & Next Steps

✓ Utilize **industry standards** to improve AV design accuracy.

✓ Continue refining AV CAD drawings with proper documentation practices.

✓ Prepare for Chapter 12: **Advanced AV CAD Techniques & Automation**.

Chapter 12: Advanced AV CAD Techniques & Automation

Automating AV CAD Workflows

The Role of Automation in AV CAD

Automation improves efficiency by reducing manual repetitive tasks in AV design. Key automation techniques include:

- **AutoLISP scripts** for automating commands
- **Dynamo for AutoCAD** to create parametric design automation
- **Batch processing tools** for modifying multiple drawings at once

Using AutoLISP for AV Design

AutoLISP scripts can:

- Automatically place AV devices based on predefined rules
- Generate cable schedules and point-to-point diagrams
- Auto-dimension rack elevations and floor plans

Creating AI-Assisted AutoCAD Macros

Using AI-driven tools, you can:

- Auto-adjust cable runs for shortest distances
- Optimize speaker placement based on room acoustics
- Detect clashes between AV and MEP systems

Hands-on Exercise

Objective: Create an AutoLISP script to automate device placement in an AV layout.

Steps:

1. Open AutoCAD and create a new LISP file.
2. Write a script to auto-insert speakers in a room layout.
3. Run the script and adjust placement based on results.
4. Save the script as **AV_AutoLISP_12.lsp**.

Quiz

1. What are the benefits of using AutoLISP in AutoCAD?

2. How does AI-assisted automation improve AV design workflows?

3. What AutoCAD feature allows for batch processing of multiple drawings?

4. What is the primary function of Dynamo in AutoCAD?

5. How can automation improve AV signal flow documentation?

Conclusion & Next Steps

✅ Implement **AutoLISP and AI-driven automation** in AV CAD workflows.

✅ Experiment with **batch processing for efficiency**.

✅ Prepare for Chapter 13: **AutoCAD Troubleshooting & Optimization**.

Chapter 13: AutoCAD Troubleshooting & Optimization

Common AutoCAD Issues in AV Design

Performance Optimization Techniques

- **Use Purge (PURGE)**: Removes unused layers, blocks, and line types.
- **Audit & Repair (AUDIT)**: Detects and fixes drawing errors.
- **Optimize File Size (OVERKILL)**: Deletes duplicate and overlapping objects.
- **Enable Hardware Acceleration**: Improves AutoCAD's performance with GPUs.

Troubleshooting Common Errors

- **Missing Xrefs**: Ensure reference paths are correct.
- **Slow Performance**: Reduce excessive hatch patterns and linework.
- **Display Issues**: Adjust graphics settings for better rendering.

Best Practices for Managing Large AV Drawings

- Use **XREFs** instead of inserting large drawings.
- Work in **Model Space** and organize views in **Paper Space**.
- Utilize **layer management** to simplify editing and navigation.

Hands-on Exercise

Objective: Optimize an AV drawing by reducing file size and improving performance.

Steps:

1. Run PURGE to remove unused items.
2. Use AUDIT to check for and fix errors.
3. Apply OVERKILL to eliminate duplicate entities.
4. Save the optimized drawing as **AV_Optimized_13.dwg**.

Quiz

1. What AutoCAD command removes unused objects from a drawing?

2. How does AUDIT help in troubleshooting?

3. What are the benefits of using XREFs instead of inserting large drawings?

4. How does enabling hardware acceleration improve AutoCAD performance?

5. What steps can you take to optimize file size in AutoCAD?

Conclusion & Next Steps

✅ Apply **troubleshooting techniques** to enhance AutoCAD efficiency.

✅ Maintain **clean, optimized AV drawings**.

✅ Prepare for Chapter 14: **Future Trends in AV System Design**.

AV & AutoCAD Definitions (2025)

This section provides key definitions related to AV technology and AutoCAD as of 2025. These definitions serve as a reference for professionals in the AV design and drafting industries.

AV Definitions (2025)

1. **4K & 8K Resolution** – Ultra-high-definition display resolutions commonly used in AV systems.

2. **AI-Assisted AV Design** – The use of artificial intelligence to optimize AV layouts and signal flow.

3. **Augmented Reality (AR) in AV** – Integration of AR technology for virtual installations and real-time visualization.

4. **AV-over-IP (AVoIP)** – A method of transmitting audiovisual signals over standard network infrastructure.

5. **Beamforming Microphone Arrays** – Advanced microphone technology that enhances speech clarity and reduces noise.

6. **Cloud-Based AV Management** – Remote monitoring and control of AV systems using cloud computing.

7. **Dante Audio Networking** – A digital audio transmission protocol used for high-quality AV installations.

8. **Hybrid Meeting Technology** – Systems designed to support both in-person and remote participants.

9. **Interactive Touch Displays** – Touch-enabled screens used for collaborative and educational applications.

10. **Projection Mapping** – The technique of projecting video content onto surfaces for immersive experiences.

AutoCAD Definitions (2025)

1. **AutoLISP Automation** – A programming language used to automate tasks in AutoCAD.

2. **BIM Integration in AutoCAD** – The use of Building Information Modeling (BIM) within AutoCAD for improved design collaboration.

3. **Cloud Collaboration in AutoCAD** – The ability to share and edit CAD drawings in real time via cloud platforms.

4. **Dynamic Blocks** – Smart blocks that adjust their shape and size based on user input.

5. **Generative Design** – AI-driven design processes that explore multiple solutions automatically.

6. **Parametric Design** – The ability to define objects and relationships mathematically for automated updates.

7. **Revit Interoperability** – Enhanced workflows between AutoCAD and Revit for architectural and AV projects.

8. **Smart Layer Management** – AI-powered suggestions for organizing layers efficiently.

9. **VR Modeling in AutoCAD** – Using virtual reality tools for immersive 3D design.

10. **XREF Cloud Integration** – The ability to use external references (XREFs) stored in cloud environments.

This section ensures that professionals are equipped with up-to-date terminology in the AV and AutoCAD industries.

Additional Topics for a Basic AutoCAD Course

Understanding the AutoCAD Interface

AutoCAD's interface is designed for efficiency and customization, helping users navigate through tools, commands, and settings effectively.

Explanation of the Ribbon, Toolbars, and Workspaces

- **Ribbon:** A visual toolbar that organizes commands into tabs and panels, making it easy to find frequently used tools.

- **Toolbars:** Traditional interface elements that can be customized for quick access to tools.

- **Workspaces:** Pre-configured layouts that adjust the interface based on different tasks, such as 2D drafting or 3D modeling.

How to Customize the Interface for Efficiency

- Rearranging toolbars and panels for easier access.

- Creating custom command aliases and shortcuts.

- Using workspace settings to save preferred layouts.

Navigating the Command Line and Status Bar

- **Command Line:** Allows users to input commands directly and see system feedback.

- **Status Bar:** Provides toggles for essential drafting settings like snap, grid, and ortho mode.

Essential Drawing Techniques

Mastering fundamental drawing tools is crucial for precision and accuracy in AutoCAD.

Using Object Snaps and Grid Settings

- **Object Snaps (OSNAP):** Helps in accurately selecting specific points like endpoints, midpoints, and intersections.

- **Grid Settings:** Provides a visual reference to help align objects properly.

Drawing Precise Lines and Shapes

- Using Line, Circle, Arc, Rectangle, and Polygon commands.
- Utilizing Dynamic Input to enter exact values.
- Snapping to predefined angles and distances.

Working with Different Coordinate Systems

- Absolute Coordinates: Based on a fixed origin (0,0).
- Relative Coordinates: Referencing previous points using @X,Y.
- Polar Coordinates: Defining points using angles and distances.

Advanced Object Manipulation

Understanding how to manipulate objects efficiently increases drawing accuracy and productivity.

Grouping and Ungrouping Objects

- Grouping objects to move, copy, and edit them together.
- Ungrouping for individual editing.

Using the Properties Palette Effectively

- Modifying object attributes such as color, layer, linetype, and dimensions.
- Adjusting properties dynamically for multiple objects.

Using Selection Methods

- Window Selection: Selects objects entirely within the window.
- Crossing Selection: Selects objects touching the selection box.
- Fence, Lasso, and Quick Select: Advanced selection methods for complex drawings.

Layer Management Best Practices

Efficient layer management improves drawing clarity and organization.

Creating, Editing, and Organizing Layers

- Assigning different objects to layers for better control.
- Using Layer Manager to modify settings.

Using Layer States to Control Visibility

- Saving different layer configurations for specific tasks.
- Turning layers on/off or freezing/thawing to improve performance.

Setting Up Color, Linetype, and Lineweight

- Assigning unique colors and line weights to differentiate objects.
- Defining custom line types for specialized drawings.

Blocks, Attributes, and Xrefs

Using reusable objects and external references reduces repetitive work.

Creating and Using Blocks for Efficiency

- Defining blocks for common objects like doors, furniture, or electrical symbols.
- Using dynamic blocks for scalable and adjustable components.

Understanding Attribute Definitions and Extracting Data

- Adding attributes (text-based data) to blocks.
- Extracting attribute data into tables or Excel for reporting.

Working with External References (Xrefs)

- Attaching Xrefs to manage large drawings.
- Updating referenced files automatically without modifying the main drawing.

Annotation and Dimensioning

Annotations make drawings more readable and provide necessary measurements.

Configuring Text Styles and Multiline Text (MText)

- Text Styles: Customizing font, size, and justification.
- MText: Allows multiline formatting with bullet points, tables, and styles.

Adding Dimensions and Controlling Styles

- Using linear, aligned, angular, radius, and ordinate dimensions.

- Setting up dimension styles for uniform annotation.

Working with Leaders and Callouts

- Leaders: Arrows pointing to key details.

- Callouts: Annotating parts of the drawing with descriptive notes.

Hatching and Gradients

Filling enclosed areas with patterns enhances visual clarity.

Applying Hatch Patterns to Enclosed Areas

- Using solid, gradient, or pattern hatches for different surfaces.

- Associating hatches with specific layers.

Adjusting Hatch Scaling and Orientation

- Modifying hatch scale and angle for better representation.

- Matching hatches across different objects.

Using Gradient Fills for Presentation Drawings

- Applying gradient fills to enhance visualization in presentation drawings.

- Combining hatch patterns with transparency effects.

Printing and Plotting Techniques

Proper plotting ensures accurate and professional-looking prints.

Setting Up Plot Styles and Layouts

- Plot Styles (CTB/STB): Assigning colors and line weights for printing.

- Using layout tabs to prepare printable sheets.

Configuring Paper Space vs. Model Space

- Model Space: Where the actual drawing is created.

- Paper Space: Used for setting up sheets, annotations, and scaling.

Printing to Scale and Exporting to PDF

- Ensuring correct scale settings for accurate prints.

- Exporting drawings to PDF for easy sharing and documentation.

Introduction to 3D Modeling (Optional for Beginners)

Basic 3D tools allow users to visualize designs in a more realistic way.

Understanding the Basics of 3D Workspaces

- Switching to 3D modeling workspace for solid modeling tools.
- Navigating with ViewCube and Orbit commands.

Creating and Modifying 3D Objects

- Extrude: Extending 2D shapes into 3D.
- Revolve: Rotating a 2D profile around an axis.
- Loft: Blending shapes along a path.

Viewing and Navigating in 3D

- Using isometric views for better visualization.
- Applying shading and rendering techniques.

Best Practices for Productivity

Increasing efficiency with time-saving tools and techniques.

Using AutoCAD Shortcuts and Custom Commands

- Customizing keyboard shortcuts for frequently used commands.
- Creating custom macros to automate tasks.

Automating Repetitive Tasks with Macros and Scripts

- Writing AutoLISP or VBA scripts to speed up repetitive operations.
- Using parametric constraints for intelligent object relationships.

Managing File Versions and Backups

- Setting up autosave and backup options.
- Using Sheet Sets to manage multiple drawings in large projects.

Basic Troubleshooting and Performance Optimization

Keeping AutoCAD running smoothly by addressing common issues.

Fixing Common Issues

- **Regenerating drawings to fix missing graphics.**

- **Restoring missing toolbars or workspace settings.**

Optimizing AutoCAD for Performance

- **Enabling hardware acceleration for faster rendering.**

- **Cleaning up unused blocks, layers, and line types to reduce file size.**

Using Recovery Tools for Corrupt Files

- **Using Drawing Recovery Manager to restore lost work.**

- **Repairing corrupt files with Audit and Purge commands.**

In AutoCAD, the Options Dialog Box contains multiple tabs that allow users to customize their settings. Below is a detailed list of all the tabs in the Options dialog box under the Profiles or Options tab.

List of Tabs in the AutoCAD Options Dialog Box

1. **Files Tab**

   - Manages file paths for templates, plot styles, support files, and external references (Xrefs).
   - Customizes AutoCAD's search paths for smooth operation.

2. **Display Tab**

   - Adjusts screen appearance, crosshair size, background color, and window behavior.
   - Controls display settings for layouts and visual effects.

3. **Open and Save Tab**

   - Configures default file save formats (e.g., AutoCAD 2024, 2018, or older versions).
   - Sets automatic save intervals and recovery options.

4. **Plot and Publish Tab**

   - Defines printing and plotting settings, including default plot styles and page setups.
   - Configures batch plotting and PDF output preferences.

5. **System Tab**

   - Controls performance-related settings like hardware acceleration and memory usage.
   - Manages external device support and hardware configurations.

6. **User Preferences Tab**

   - Customizes cursor behavior, right-click settings, and selection modes.
   - Configures default double-click actions.

7. **Drafting Tab**

   - Adjusts object snap, grid, and polar tracking settings.

- Configures AutoSnap features for precision drawing.

8. **3D Modeling Tab**

   - Controls visual styles, 3D navigation settings, and performance optimization for 3D workspaces.

   - Configures smoothness settings for 3D objects.

9. **Selection Tab**

   - Sets selection highlighting, grips display, and object selection preferences.

   - Adjusts selection preview and cycling settings.

10. **Profiles Tab**

- Stores user profiles, including all customized settings and preferences.

- Allows exporting and importing profiles (.arg files) for easy migration.

Detailed Breakdown Options Dialog Box Tab

1. Files Tab

The Files tab is where AutoCAD manages paths and directories for various system functions. It helps configure locations for essential files.

Key Settings:

- **Support File Search Path** – Specifies directories where AutoCAD looks for required files (e.g., fonts, hatch patterns).

- **Working Support File Search Path** – Defines additional folders where custom support files can be stored.

- **Device Driver File Search Path** – Points to drivers required for external devices like plotters and digitizers.

- **Customization Files Location** – Stores .cuix (menu customization) files for personalized toolbars and workspaces.

- **Automatic Save File Location** – Defines where AutoCAD saves backup files (.sv$).

- **Template File Location** – Specifies the default location for drawing templates (.dwt).

- **Plot Style Table Search Path** – Sets the location for CTB and STB plot style files used for printing.

- **Printer Configuration Search Path** – Defines paths for PC3 files, which store plotter settings.

- **Log File Location** – Stores log files generated by AutoCAD for troubleshooting.

2. Display Tab

The Display tab controls the appearance of AutoCAD's interface and workspace.

Key Settings:

- **Window Elements**

  - **Crosshair Size** – Adjusts the crosshair percentage of screen coverage.

  - **Color Scheme** – Switches between Light or Dark Mode for AutoCAD's theme.

  - **Display Scroll Bars in Drawing Window** – Enables or disables scroll bars for navigation.

- **Display Resolution**

  - **Arc and Circle Smoothness** – Controls the appearance of curves and arcs.

  - **Line Weight Display** – Toggles visibility of line weights in Model Space.

- **Layout Elements**

  - **Display Paper Background** – Simulates paper appearance in Layout (Paper Space).

  - **Show Page Setup Manager for New Layouts** – Allows users to configure layouts before use.

---

3. Open and Save Tab

This tab sets default save formats, autosave intervals, and recovery options to prevent data loss.

Key Settings:

- **File Save**

  - **Save As Type** – Determines the default file format (e.g., AutoCAD 2024, 2018, etc.).

  - **Maintain Drawing List** – Keeps a record of recently opened files.

- **Autosave and Security**

  - **Automatic Save** – Enables automatic file backup at set intervals.

  - **File Safety Precautions** – Prompts users before overwriting files.

- **Demand Loading of Xrefs** – Controls how external references (.dwg) load (full, partial, or disabled).

- **Object ARX Applications – Manages external add-ins used for automation.**

---

4. Plot and Publish Tab

The Plot and Publish tab manages plotting settings, batch printing, and default output configurations.

Key Settings:

- **Plot Options**
    - **Add/Modify Plotters – Allows configuration of new printers or plotters.**
    - **Default Output Format – Selects PDF, DWG, or another output format.**

- **Background Processing**
    - **Plot in Background – Enables multitasking by processing plots in the background.**
    - **Publish in Background – Allows AutoCAD to continue working while publishing multiple layouts.**

- **Plot Style Tables**
    - **Use Color-Dependent Plot Styles (CTB) or Named Plot Styles (STB) – Defines how objects print based on color or assigned styles.**

---

5. System Tab

This tab contains system-level settings that affect overall AutoCAD performance and compatibility.

Key Settings:

- **Performance Tuning**
    - **Enable Hardware Acceleration – Uses GPU for faster processing.**
    - **Cache Model Tab and Layouts – Improves drawing performance.**

- **Graphics Performance**
    - **Smooth Line Display – Enhances line clarity.**
    - **Hardware Acceleration – Boosts speed for 3D and large files.**

- **Startup Settings**

- o **Show Welcome Screen – Toggles startup tips and tutorials.**
- o **Single Document Mode – Limits AutoCAD to one open drawing at a time.**
- **External Devices**
  - o **Digitizer Settings – Configures external input devices like drawing tablets.**

6. User Preferences Tab

Controls interface behavior and user experience settings.

Key Settings:

- **Right-Click Customization**
  - o **Default Mode – Enables right-click to function as Enter.**
  - o **Edit Mode – Allows right-click for context-sensitive menus.**
- **Windows Standard Behavior**
  - o **Double-Click Editing – Enables quick edits on objects.**
  - o **Shortcut Menus – Activates pop-up menus for selected objects.**
- **Hyperlink Behavior**
  - o **Enable URL Hyperlinks – Allows links in drawings.**

7. Drafting Tab

This tab fine-tunes drafting aids and precision tools.

Key Settings:

- **Object Snap Options**
  - o **Enable Object Snaps (OSNAP) – Toggles snapping to key points.**
  - o **AutoSnap Marker Size – Adjusts snap cursor size.**
- **Grid and Polar Tracking**
  - o **Grid Display – Controls grid visibility.**
  - o **Polar Tracking Angles – Defines snap angles for alignment.**

- **Dynamic Input**

  - **Show Command Prompt in Drawing Area – Enables on-screen command entry.**

---

8. 3D Modeling Tab

This tab focuses on 3D workspaces, visual styles, and performance settings.

Key Settings:

- **3D Workspace Settings**

  - **Display the ViewCube – Toggles the 3D navigation cube.**

  - **Enable SteeringWheels – Activates quick 3D navigation.**

- **Rendering and Visualization**

  - **Visual Styles – Controls shading and lighting.**

  - **Smoothness and Resolution – Defines quality of 3D curves.**

- **Performance**

  - **Use High-Quality Geometry – Improves rendering.**

---

9. Selection Tab

Controls how objects are selected within AutoCAD.

Key Settings:

- **Selection Preview**

  - **Highlight Objects on Hover – Shows preview before selection.**

  - **Cycle Selection – Enables toggling through overlapping objects.**

- **Grip Display**

  - **Show Grips on Selected Objects – Enables easy object manipulation.**

---

10. Profiles Tab

The Profiles tab allows users to save, load, and manage AutoCAD configurations.

Key Settings:

- **Current Profile**
  - ○ **Displays the active AutoCAD profile.**

- **Import/Export Profile**
  - ○ **Allows saving profiles as .arg files to transfer settings.**

- **Reset Profile**
  - ○ **Restores default AutoCAD settings.**

Using These Tabs Effectively

1. **Customize Workspaces – Adjust interface settings under Display & User Preferences tabs.**

2. **Optimize Performance – Use System, 3D Modeling, and Drafting tabs to tweak AutoCAD speed.**

3. **Save Time on Repetitive Tasks – Configure default file paths and settings in the Files and Open/Save tabs.**

4. **Improve Printing Quality – Fine-tune Plot and Publish settings to match project requirements.**

5. **Backup and Restore Settings – Use the Profiles tab to save and reload configurations.**

AutoCAD Commands List

Basic Commands:

LINE (L) - Draws a straight line segment.

PLINE (PL) - Creates a polyline.

CIRCLE (C) - Draws a circle.

ARC (A) - Draws an arc.

RECTANGLE (REC) - Draws a rectangle.

ELLIPSE (EL) - Draws an ellipse.

TEXT (T) - Adds text to a drawing.

MTEXT (MT) - Creates multiline text.

HATCH (H) - Fills an enclosed area with a pattern.

DIM (D) - Adds dimensions to a drawing.

Editing Commands:

ERASE (E) - Deletes objects.

COPY (CO) - Duplicates objects.

MOVE (M) - Moves objects to a new location.

ROTATE (RO) - Rotates objects.

SCALE (SC) - Changes the size of an object.

MIRROR (MI) - Creates a mirrored copy of an object.

TRIM (TR) - Trims objects to a cutting edge.

EXTEND (EX) - Extends an object to meet another object.

OFFSET (O) - Creates parallel copies of objects.

FILLET (F) - Rounds the edges of objects.

CHAMFER (CHA) - Bevels the edges of objects.

Workflow and Best Practices

Drawing Aids and Inquiry Commands:

OSNAP (OS) - Sets object snap modes.

GRID (F7) - Toggles the display grid.

ORTHO (F8) - Restricts movement to horizontal or vertical directions.

SNAP (F9) - Toggles snap mode.

ZOOM (Z) - Adjusts the view of the drawing.

PAN (P) - Moves the view of the drawing.

DIST (DI) - Measures the distance between two points.

LIST (LI) - Displays information about objects.

ID (ID) - Identifies a point's coordinates.

Layers and Properties Commands:

LAYER (LA) - Manages layers.

PROPERTIES (CH, PR) - Displays object properties.

MATCHPROP (MA) - Matches properties between objects.

CHANGE (CH) - Changes properties of objects.

COLOR (COL) - Sets the current color.

Block and Group Commands:

BLOCK (B) - Creates a block.

INSERT (I) - Inserts a block.

EXPLODE (X) - Breaks a block into separate objects.

WBLOCK (WB) - Writes objects to a new drawing file.

GROUP (G) - Groups objects together.

UNGROUP (UNG) - Ungroups objects.

Advanced Commands:

XREF (XR) - Manages external references.

ATTDEF (ATT) - Defines attributes.

ATTEDIT (ATE) - Edits block attributes.

TABLE (TB) - Creates a table.

MTEXTEDIT (ED) - Edits multiline text.

MLEADER (MLD) - Creates a leader with an annotation.

SPLINE (SPL) - Creates a smooth curve.

REVOLVE (REV) - Creates a 3D solid by revolving an object.

EXTRUDE (EXT) - Converts a 2D shape into a 3D solid.

File Management Commands:

SAVE (QSAVE) - Saves the current drawing.

SAVEAS (SA) - Saves the drawing under a new name.

OPEN (O) - Opens an existing drawing.

NEW (N) - Starts a new drawing.

EXPORT (EXP) - Exports objects to other file formats.

IMPORT (IM) - Imports files into the drawing.

PLOT (PLO) - Prints the drawing.

AutoCAD Menu Bar Items and Their Functions

File Menu

New (CTRL+N) - Opens a new drawing file.

Open (CTRL+O) - Opens an existing drawing.

Save (CTRL+S) - Saves the current drawing.

Save As - Saves the drawing under a different name or format.

Export - Allows exporting the drawing in other formats (e.g., PDF, DWG, DWF).

Print (PLOT) - Prints or plots the drawing.

Close - Closes the current drawing.

Exit - Exits AutoCAD.

Edit Menu

Undo (CTRL+Z) - Reverses the last action.

Redo (CTRL+Y) - Reapplies the last undone action.

Cut (CTRL+X) - Removes and copies selected objects.

Copy (CTRL+C) - Copies selected objects.

Paste (CTRL+V) - Pastes copied objects.

Delete - Removes selected objects from the drawing.

View Menu

Zoom - Adjusts the view to focus on specific areas.

Pan - Moves the view within the drawing.

Orbit - Rotates the view in a 3D environment.

Regenerate - Refreshes the drawing display.

Visual Styles - Changes the appearance of 3D objects.

Layer Properties Manager - Manages drawing layers.

Insert Menu

Block - Inserts a pre-defined block.

Xref (External Reference) - Attaches external DWG files.

Raster Image - Inserts image files into the drawing.

Attach PDF - Embeds PDF files.

Table - Creates and inserts tables.

AutoCAD Palettes and Their Uses for Beginners

Tool Palettes

Purpose

Provides a customizable interface for frequently used tools and commands.

How to Use

- Open by typing TOOLPALETTES or pressing CTRL+3.

- Drag and drop commands or blocks onto the palette for quick access.

- Customize and create new palettes by right-clicking on the palette window.

Properties Palette

Purpose

Displays and allows modification of object properties.

How to Use

- Open by typing PROPERTIES or pressing CTRL+1.

- Select an object to view and edit its properties, such as layer, color, and dimensions.

- Useful for making quick changes to multiple objects at once.

Layer Properties Manager Palette

Purpose

Manages layers for organizing drawing components.

How to Use

- Open by typing LAYER or pressing LA.

- Create, rename, and manage layers to control object visibility and organization.

- Set layer properties such as color, linetype, and transparency.

Design Center Palette

Purpose

Provides access to blocks, layers, and other drawing components from external files.

How to Use

- Open by typing **ADCENTER** or pressing **CTRL+2.**

- Drag objects from existing drawings into the current project.

- Organize and reuse design elements efficiently.

AutoCAD Keyboard Shortcuts List

Basic Drawing Shortcuts

L - Line

PL - Polyline

C - Circle

A - Arc

REC - Rectangle

EL - Ellipse

T - Single Line Text

MT - Multiline Text

H - Hatch

D - Dimension

Editing Shortcuts

E - Erase

CO - Copy

M - Move

RO - Rotate

SC - Scale

MI - Mirror

TR - Trim

EX - Extend

O - Offset

F - Fillet

CHA - Chamfer

View and Navigation Shortcuts

Z - Zoom

P - Pan

RE - Regenerate

Workflow and Best Practices

F7 - Grid Toggle

F8 - Ortho Mode Toggle

F9 - Snap Mode Toggle

F3 - Object Snap Toggle

F6 - Dynamic UCS Toggle

F12 - Dynamic Input Toggle

Object Properties and Layers Shortcuts

LA - Layer Properties Manager

CH / PR - Change Properties

MA - Match Properties

CUI - Customize User Interface

Block and Group Shortcuts

B - Create Block

I - Insert Block

X - Explode Block

WB - Write Block

G - Group

UNG - Ungroup

Annotation Shortcuts

LE - Leader

MLD - Multileader

DLI - Linear Dimension

DAL - Aligned Dimension

DDI - Diameter Dimension

DRA - Radius Dimension

DIM - Dimension Style Manager

MTEXTEDIT - Edit Multiline Text

Advanced Commands Shortcuts

XREF - Manage External References

ATT - Define Attributes

ATE - Edit Attributes

TB - Create Table

SPL - Spline

REV - Revolve (3D)

EXT - Extrude (3D)

File Management Shortcuts

Q - Quick Save

QSAVE - Save Drawing

SA - Save As

O - Open Drawing

N - New Drawing

EXP - Export Drawing

IM - Import File

PLOT - Print Drawing

Reference Materials

AV Drafting Standards & Best Practices

AV Drafting Scope

This section outlines standard drafting documentation for AV system design. The following pages define the structure and contents of a complete AV drafting set:

- **AV001 - Cover Sheet:** Includes index, legends, abbreviations, and general notes.

- **AV101 - Key & Enlarged Floor Plans:** Shows major AV devices and their placements.

- **AV201 - Elevations:** Provides wall elevation views of AV equipment.

- **AV301 - Details & Equipment Rack Elevations:** Displays detailed drawings of rack-mounted AV components.

- **AV401 - Single Line Diagrams:** Covers signal flow for video, audio, control, and data.

- **AV501 - Control System User Interface Layout:** Illustrates control system configurations.

Drawing Progress Sets

To ensure a systematic approach, AV drafting progresses through the following phases:

- **30% Completion – Initial schematic design (SD)**

- **60% Completion – Design development (DD)**

- **90% Completion – Pre-final construction documents (CD)**

- **100% Completion – Finalized construction documents**

Layer Naming & Standards

For organization and clarity, all AV-related components are assigned standardized layers, including:

- **Devices (displays, speakers, microphones, racks)**

- **Wiring (audio, video, control, power)**

- **Text Labels & Dimensions (annotations, callouts, dimensions)**

Title Block & External References

- Use a standardized title block across all drawings.
- Maintain external references (XREFs) to link architectural, electrical, and structural backgrounds into AutoCAD.

Plotting & File Management

- Standard Plotting Settings: Utilize Monochrome.ctb for black-and-white output to maintain consistency.
- File Structure Recommendations:
  - Admin – Project administration documents.
  - Source – Original architectural and engineering drawings.
  - Production – Working AutoCAD/Revit files.
  - References – Background files, title blocks, and logos.
  - Output – Final PDF sets and issued drawings.

CAD File Request & Coordination

For AV system integration, precise coordination with architectural drawings is essential. Requests for CAD files should include:

- Floor plans
- Reflected ceiling plans
- Elevations & sections
- Furniture layouts
- Title blocks with necessary project details

Managing AutoCAD Layers for AV Integration

- Ensure furniture, lighting fixtures, HVAC ducts/vents, and ceiling features are included in AV drawings.
- Define positioning methods when linking architectural Revit models (origin, base point, center, etc.).

AV System Design Standards & Room Types

Standard AV System Components

- **Displays: Flat panels, projectors, confidence monitors.**

- **Sound: Ceiling speakers, soundbars, microphone arrays.**

- **Conferencing: PTZ cameras, wireless microphones, Zoom Room PCs.**

- **Control: Touch panels, button controllers, AV-over-IP systems.**

- **Infrastructure: Equipment racks, lecterns, cable management solutions.**

Common Room Types & Configurations

- **Classrooms: Standard, distance learning, active learning, and labs.**

- **Conference Rooms: Large, medium, and huddle spaces.**

- **AV Cart & Digital Signage: Portable AV setups for flexible spaces.**

AV Cost Considerations

- **Installation Costs: Consideration of infrastructure, labor, and support.**

- **Cost-efficient Integration Strategies: Prioritizing scalable solutions and long-term maintenance.**

Advanced CAD Automation & BIM Integration

Automating AV Workflows

- **AutoLISP scripting: Automates device placement and cable routing in AutoCAD.**

- **Batch Processing: Enhances efficiency by modifying multiple drawings simultaneously.**

- **Dynamo Scripting for BIM: Facilitates parametric automation in Revit.**

- **AI-Assisted Layout Optimization: Uses AI tools for automated space planning and clash detection.**

AutoCAD Troubleshooting & Optimization

Common AutoCAD Issues in AV Design

- **Missing XREFs: Ensure correct reference paths.**

- **Slow Performance: Reduce excessive hatches and complex linework.**

- **Display Issues: Adjust graphics settings and viewport scaling.**

Optimization Techniques

- **Using PURGE: Removes unused layers, blocks, and line types.**

- **Running AUDIT: Detects and fixes errors within the drawing.**

- **Applying OVERKILL: Deletes duplicate and overlapping objects to improve efficiency.**

This reference section serves as a guide to streamlining AV CAD workflows, optimizing drafting processes, and ensuring accuracy in AV system documentation.

Enhancing AV CAD & System Design

Innovation and Best Practices

This section of the book serves as a comprehensive guide to modern AV CAD workflows, real-world project applications, and industry best practices. It provides practical insights, case studies, and interactive elements to elevate your understanding of AV system design and implementation.

---

1. Real-World Case Studies

Bringing real-life experience into AV CAD & System Design, this section presents detailed breakdowns of successful AV projects in different industries:

Corporate Boardrooms

- Designing AV layouts for high-profile corporate clients using video conferencing systems, interactive displays, and audio enhancement tools.

- Reference Materials:
    - AVIXA AV Design Reference Manual
    - Crestron Conference Room AV Guidelines
    - Cisco Webex Room Integration Guide

Educational Institutions

- Implementing hybrid learning solutions with lecture hall AV systems, smart podiums, and networked AV distribution.

- Reference Materials:
    - Extron Classroom AV System Design Guide
    - AVIXA Classroom Acoustics Standards
    - Dante Networked AV for Education

Entertainment & Hospitality Venues

- Case studies on video walls, projection mapping, and immersive AV experiences in hotels, casinos, and concert halls.

- Reference Materials:
  - Christie Digital Projection Mapping Guide
  - AVIXA Large Venue AV Installation Guide
  - Meyer Sound Concert Audio System Design

Government & Public Spaces

- AV integration for courtrooms, city council chambers, public safety command centers, and emergency broadcast systems.

- Reference Materials:
  - Biamp Courtroom AV Solutions
  - AVIXA Public Safety and Government AV Guidelines
  - Crestron City Hall & Courtroom AV System Design

Before & After Comparisons

- How AV upgrades transform spaces with improved workflow efficiency, enhanced audience engagement, and automation.

---

2. Exclusive AV CAD Workflows

This section provides proprietary AutoCAD and Revit workflows to streamline AV system design.

Step-by-Step Guide

- Covers the full AV CAD drawing process from concept sketches to final construction documentation.

- Reference Materials:
  - Autodesk AutoCAD Electrical User Guide
  - AVIXA Signal Flow and Rack Elevation Standards

Template Libraries

- **Custom CAD blocks for racks, projectors, microphones, speakers, displays, and control panels.**

- **Reference Materials:**

  - **Crestron AV Rack CAD Blocks**

  - **Extron Connector and Cable CAD Symbols**

  - **Biamp Audio DSP Design Templates**

Automation Techniques

- **How to use AutoLISP, Revit Dynamo scripting, and BIM automation to accelerate drawing workflows.**

- **Reference Materials:**

  - **Autodesk Dynamo for Revit Automation**

  - **AutoLISP Programming for AutoCAD AV Design**

---

3. Industry Best Practices & Standards

Ensuring AV designs meet compliance, safety, and integration standards.

AVIXA Guidelines

- **Signal flow documentation, AV network design, and equipment placement best practices.**

- **Reference Materials:**

  - **AVIXA CTS-D Certification Guide**

  - **AVIXA Audio and Video System Design Standards**

NFPA 72 Fire Alarm Code

- **Integrating fire alarm considerations in AV design, such as ensuring proper audio evacuation system installation.**

- **Reference Materials:**

  - **NFPA 72 National Fire Alarm and Signaling Code**

  - **OSHA Fire Protection Engineering Guidelines**

ADA Compliance

- Guidelines for accessible AV systems in public spaces.
- Reference Materials:
    - ADA Compliance Standards for AV Systems
    - AVIXA Accessible Technology Guidelines

IEEE & ANSI Standards

- Documentation best practices for cabling, grounding, and electrical safety.
- Reference Materials:
    - IEEE Standard 802.3 Ethernet for AV over IP
    - ANSI Audio and Video Equipment Testing Standards

---

4. Digital Extras & Interactive Elements

Interactive resources:

- Direct links to demonstrations of AV CAD workflows.
- Reference Materials:
    - Autodesk AutoCAD Electrical Video Guide
    - Extron AV System Setup Tutorials

Downloadable Templates & Checklists

- Ready-to-use AV CAD blocks, signal flow diagrams, and system schematics.

5. Business & Career Growth for AV Professionals

How to leverage AV CAD expertise for business success.

Starting an AV CAD Consulting Business

- Steps to launch a freelance or full-time AV CAD business.
- Reference Materials:
    - AVIXA AV Business Best Practices Guide
    - NSCA AV Integrator Business Growth Handbook

Freelancing & Subcontracting

- How to secure contracts and partnerships with AV integrators.

Collaboration with Architects & IT Teams

- The role of AV designers in large-scale construction projects.

---

6. AI & Automation in AV System Design

The future of AV technology and how AI is shaping AV CAD workflows.

AI-Driven CAD Tools

- AI tools that automate AV layouts and optimize speaker placement.
- Reference Materials:
    - AI in BIM and Smart Buildings
    - Crestron AI-Controlled AV Systems

BIM (Building Information Modeling) in AV

- How BIM is transforming AV design and collaboration.
- Reference Materials:
    - Autodesk BIM for AV System Design
    - Revit BIM Integration Guide

7. Common AV Design Mistakes & Troubleshooting

Avoiding costly errors in AV integration.

Cable Management & Routing Mistakes

- Dos and don'ts in AV wiring.
- Reference Materials:
    - Extron AV Cable Management Guide
    - Belden AV Cabling Best Practices

Power & Grounding Issues

- Preventing hum, buzz, and signal noise.
- Reference Materials:
    - NEC Electrical Code for AV Systems
    - AVIXA Power Conditioning & Grounding Standards

---

8. Hands-On Learning: Exercises & Quizzes

Engaging self-paced learning.

Mini AV CAD Projects

- Hands-on exercises to practice AV schematics.
- Reference Materials:
    - Autodesk AutoCAD Electrical Training Guide
    - Extron Signal Flow Diagram Workbook

9. Emerging Technologies in AV System Design

Exploring the next generation of AV technology.

AV-over-IP & Networked AV Systems

- **How AV is shifting from traditional setups to networked solutions.**
- **Reference Materials:**
    - **Dante AV-over-IP Implementation Guide**
    - **AVIXA Networked AV System Design**

Wireless AV Technology

- **The rise of wireless control systems, speakers, and displays.**
- **Reference Materials:**
    - **Crestron Wireless AV Systems Guide**
    - **Biamp Wireless Microphone System Design**

Augmented Reality (AR) & Virtual Reality (VR) in AV

- **The role of immersive AV in interactive installations.**
- **Reference Materials:**
    - **Epson AR/VR Projection Technology**
    - **AVIXA Extended Reality (XR) in AV Design**

Drawing Set Releases and Revisions

Overview

This document outlines the workflow for releasing drawing sets and documenting revisions at Alegeh Drafting and Consulting. The goal is to streamline the process and maintain consistency across all project documentation.

Drawing Set Releases

Drawing Set Releases involve publishing the entire set of drawings during the design phase. These releases compile all known changes and present them as a comprehensive set, such as 50% CD, 75% CD, 100% CD, or Issued for Construction (IFC).

Note: The naming of different design sets may vary from project to project. In some cases, it will be determined by the client or architect, while in others, Alegeh Drafting and Consulting may define the naming conventions.

During larger projects, drawings may be released in phases. For instance, video drawings may be released first, followed by audio drawings. Each release should be clearly identified, such as "IFC Video" or "IFC Audio."

The final complete Drawing Set Release occurs with the As-Built set, reflecting all implemented changes and final conditions.

Drawing Revisions

Drawing revisions occur during the construction phase when updates are made after the drawing set has already been issued for implementation. Revisions are noted on the Revision Grid on each individual drawing and clearly marked with revision clouds on designated layers.

Workflow for Drawing Set Releases

1. Update the master Xref file to reflect the release name and date.

2. Update the Drawing Index to show which drawings are included in the new release.

3. Label the updated drawings accordingly to maintain clarity and documentation integrity.

Workflow for Drawing Revisions

1. Determine whether a CAD update is required and ensure the project team agrees on the revision.

2. Document the revision with an appropriate designation, such as CD -01, CD -02, etc.

3. Update the Revision Grid on each affected drawing to include the new revision information.

4. Use revision clouds to mark changes and ensure they are labeled with the revision number and description.

5. Update the Drawing Index to reflect the revised drawings included in the CD release.

6. Archive the revised drawing set in a dedicated folder named according to the CD designation.

Revision Numbering and CD Sets

It is important not to confuse individual drawing revision numbers with CD set numbers. Drawing revision numbers indicate how many times a specific drawing has been updated after being issued for construction, while CD sets represent the collection of revised drawings issued as a unit.

Example: If a router expansion requires a new patch panel, and previous changes were designated as CD -01 and CD -02, the new change would be CD -03. The rack elevation might have been previously revised under CD -01, making the new revision Rev 02. However, if it is the first revision for the patch panel elevation and router wiring diagram, it would be Rev 01.

Summary of Release and Revision Workflow

- **Drawing Set Releases during design phases: Update Xref files and Drawing Index with release names and dates.**

- **Updating Drawings during Construction: Ensure team agreement, update affected drawings with new revision numbers, mark revisions with clouds and numbering, and archive updated sets properly.**

By following these structured workflows, Alegeh Drafting and Consulting ensures accurate documentation and effective project management throughout the entire lifecycle of the project.

CAD Standards and Reference Training Guide

Overview This training guide outlines the CAD standards, guidelines, and best practices to be followed in professional environments. It serves as a comprehensive resource to maintain consistency, accuracy, and efficiency in the creation, management, and release of CAD drawings. This guide is suitable for CAD operators, project managers, and technical staff involved in drafting and documentation.

Table of Contents

1. **Introduction**
2. **CAD Standards and Guidelines**
3. **Drawing Set Releases and Revisions**
4. **AutoCAD File Formats and Standards**
5. **Plot Style Tables and Colors**
6. **Layering and Drawing Set Up**
7. **Dimensioning and Text Styles**
8. **Drawing Numbering and Naming Conventions**
9. **Rack Elevations and Signal Flow Diagrams**
10. **Documentation and Archiving**

1. Introduction

This training guide aims to provide best practices and standardized procedures essential for consistent and professional CAD deliverables. These standards are designed to be scalable for diverse projects and adaptable for client-specific requirements.

2. CAD Standards and Guidelines

All CAD drawings must adhere to standardized practices outlined here, including file naming conventions, layering, dimensioning, and text styles. Regular audits and revisions of CAD files ensure compliance and maintain quality.

3. Drawing Set Releases and Revisions

CAD drawings undergo structured releases and revisions to ensure accurate and traceable documentation. Each revision is clearly marked, and drawing sets are released in phases to maintain workflow efficiency.

Release Workflow:

1. Update the master Xref file with release name and date.

2. Adjust the Drawing Index to include new and revised drawings.

3. Clearly label each drawing to maintain documentation integrity.

Revision Workflow:

1. Agree on necessary CAD updates.

2. Document revisions with appropriate numbering (e.g., CD -01).

3. Use revision clouds to mark changes.

4. Update the Drawing Index to reflect revisions.

4. AutoCAD File Formats and Standards

All CAD files are saved in Autodesk's DWG format. Compatibility is maintained through standardized settings and templates. Following the AutoCAD 2013 standard ensures cross-platform compatibility.

5. Plot Style Tables and Colors

Drawings use a standardized plot style table to maintain consistency in line weights and colors. Base colors and extended colors are defined to ensure clarity in visual representation.

6. Layering and Drawing Set Up

Layer names follow a specific naming convention that includes a discipline designator and a description of the content. Layers are organized for easy reference and efficient management.

7. Dimensioning and Text Styles

Dimensioning and text styles are standardized to ensure legibility and consistency. Text height and line weight are adjusted according to the drawing scale.

8. Drawing Numbering and Naming Conventions

Drawing numbering follows a structured format to ensure easy reference. Numbering is based on project scope, room type, and drawing type, with distinct identifiers for each set.

9. Rack Elevations and Signal Flow Diagrams

Rack elevations are drawn to show the accurate placement of each device within a rack. Signal flow diagrams are structured to detail audio, video, and control connections clearly.

10. Documentation and Archiving

All finalized drawings and revisions are archived with complete documentation. Each archive includes the project number, drawing index, and related release notes.

By adhering to these CAD standards and guidelines, professionals can ensure quality and consistency in deliverables, enhancing efficiency and professionalism in CAD operations.

AV Project Drawings Sign-Off Checklist

Task	Status	Completed By	Date Completed	Notes
Project Initiation	Not Started			
Review Scope of Work (SOW)	Not Started			
Obtain Project Drawings and Documentation	Not Started			
Create Initial Floor Plans	Not Started			
Identify Equipment Placement	Not Started			
Develop Signal Flow Diagrams	Not Started			
Coordinate with Architects and Engineers	Not Started			
Draft Rack Elevations	Not Started			
Draft Equipment Wiring Diagrams	Not Started			
Label All Components	Not Started			
Ensure ADA and Code Compliance	Not Started			
Review with Project Manager	Not Started			
Revise Based on Feedback	Not Started			
Submit for Internal Review	Not Started			
Address Internal Review Comments	Not Started			
Submit Drawings for Client Review	Not Started			
Address Client Review Comments	Not Started			
Finalize Drawings	Not Started			
Prepare As-Built Drawings	Not Started			
Export and Format Drawings (PDF, DWG)	Not Started			
Submit Final Documentation to Client	Not Started			
Archive Project Files	Not Started			
Close Out Checklist	Not Started			

AV Drawing Index

DRAWING INDEX

NOTE: AN "X" AT INTERSECTION OF DRAWING AND RELEASE INDICATES THAT THIS DRAWING WAS INCLUDED IN THAT RELEASE. IF INTERSECTION IS BLANK, THEN DRAWING WAS NOT PART OF THAT RELEASE.

DRAWING NUMBER	DRAWING TITLE	DRAWING SET RELEASE / DATE	50% CD 2020-04-08	75% CD 2020-05-17	100% CD 2020-06-02	ISSUED FOR CONSTRUCTION 2020-07-10	ACD-01 2020-07-29	ACD-02 2020-08-02	ACD-03 2020-09-13	ACD-04 2020-10-16	AS BUILT 2020-12-19
TA00-000	AUDIOVISUAL DRAWING INDEX		X	X	X	X	X	X	X	X	X
TA00-001	AUDIOVISUAL RESPONSIBILITIES, SYMBOLS, ABBREVIATIONS AND NOTES		X	X	X	X					X
TA01-101	1ST FLOOR PLAN		X	X	X	X	X			X	X
TA01-131	CONFERENCE ROOM ELEVATION		X	X	X	X	X				X
TA01-311	CAMERAS 1 TO 6, VIDEO CABLE WIRING DIAGRAM			X	X					X	X
TA01-321	AUDIO CONF, WIRING DIAGRAM			X	X		X			X	

AV Equipment Rack

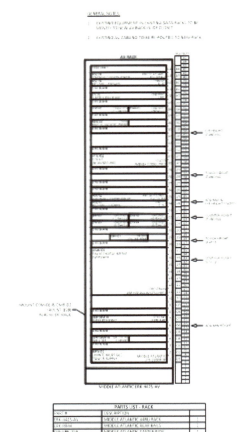

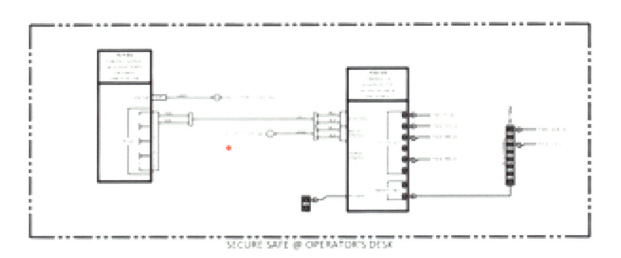

SECURE SAFE @ OPERATOR'S DESK

References

Workflow and Best Practices

AVIXA. (n.d.). *AV Design Reference Manual*. Retrieved from [AVIXA Website](#)

Biamp Systems. (n.d.). *Courtroom AV Solutions*. Retrieved from [Biamp Website](#)

Christie Digital. (n.d.). *Projection Mapping Guide*. Retrieved from [Christie Digital Website](#)

Cisco. (n.d.). *Webex Room Integration Guide*. Retrieved from [Cisco Website](#)

Crestron Electronics. (n.d.). *Conference Room AV Guidelines*. Retrieved from [Crestron Website](#)

Extron Electronics. (n.d.). *Classroom AV System Design Guide*. Retrieved from [Extron Website](#)

Meyer Sound. (n.d.). *Concert Audio System Design*. Retrieved from [Meyer Sound Website](#)

National Fire Protection Association (NFPA). (2025). *NFPA 72: National Fire Alarm and Signaling Code*. Retrieved from [NFPA Website](#)

IEEE Standards Association. (2025). *IEEE Standard 802.3: Ethernet for AV over IP*. Retrieved from [IEEE Website](#)

Autodesk. (n.d.). *AutoCAD Electrical User Guide*. Retrieved from [Autodesk Website](#)

Autodesk. (n.d.). *Dynamo for Revit Automation*. Retrieved from [Autodesk Website](#)

AVIXA. (n.d.). *CTS-D Certification Guide*. Retrieved from [AVIXA Website](#)

Extron Electronics. (n.d.). *Signal Flow Diagram Workbook*. Retrieved from [Extron Website](#)

Chapter 1
Introduction

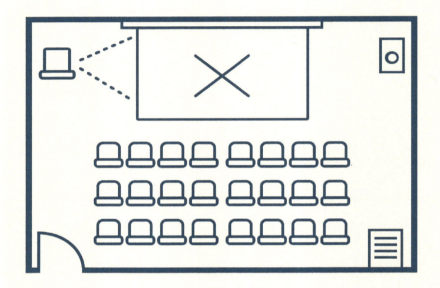

Chapter 2
System Design Principles

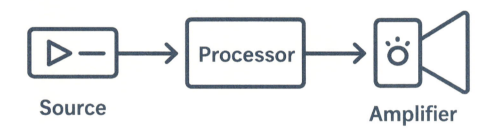

Source   Processor   Amplifier

Chapter 2
AutoCAD Essentials for AV Design

Image: Layer management interface in AutoCAD

Image: Demonstration of basic drawing commands (line, rectangle, circle)

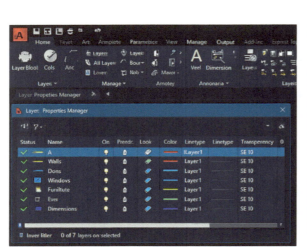

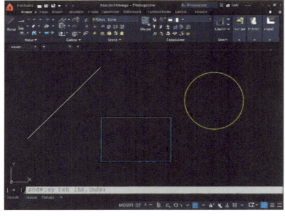

Chapter 3
Introduction to Signal Flow

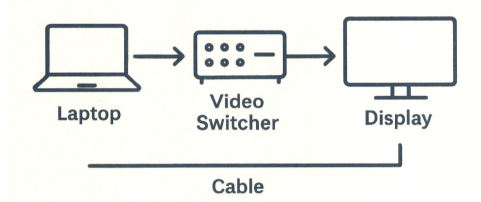

Laptop   Video Switcher   Display

Cable

CHAPTER 3: AV SYMBOLS, BLOCKS & STANDARDS

COMMON AV SYMBOLS AND THEIR USES

DISPLAY

PROJECTION SCREEN

CEILING SPEAKER

LOUDSPEAKER

CAMERA

MICROPHONE

LAPTOP

LAPTOP

CREATING AND INSERTING AV BLOCKS IN AUTOCAD

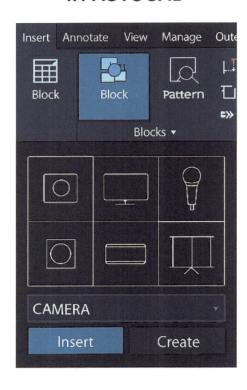

CHAPTER 4: SIGNAL FLOW DIAGRAMS & LINE TYPES

SAMPLE SIGNAL FLOW DIAGRAM FOR A CONFERENCE ROOM SETUP

LINE TYPES FOR VIDEO, AUDIO, AND CONTROL SIGNALS

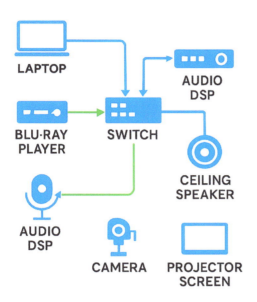

LAPTOP

AUDIO DSP

BLU·RAY PLAYER

SWITCH

CEILING SPEAKER

AUDIO DSP

CAMERA

PROJECTOR SCREEN

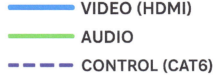

VIDEO (HDMI)

AUDIO

CONTROL (CAT6)

CONFERENCE ROOM AV DESIGN PRINCIPLES

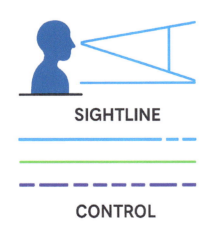

SIGHTLINE

CONTROL

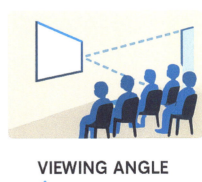

VIEWING ANGLE

CHAPTER 4
AV DESIGN PRINCIPLES

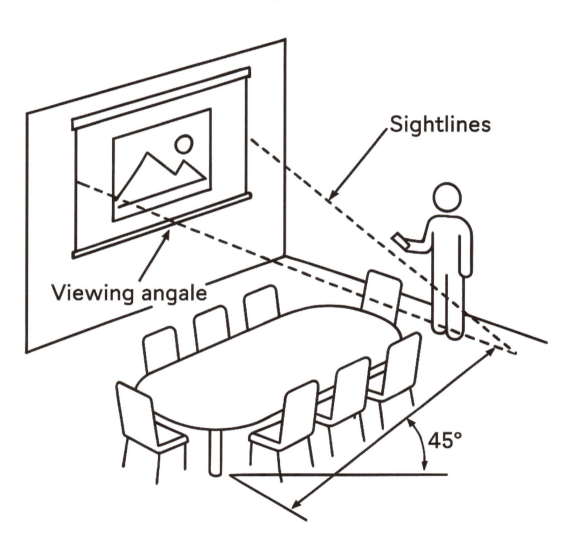

Chapter 5:
Rack Elevations & Equipment Layouts

Example of a 12U AV rack layout with labeled equipmet

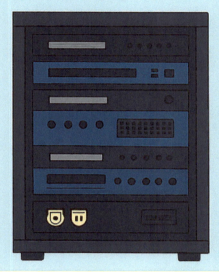

Cable management best practices in a rack setup

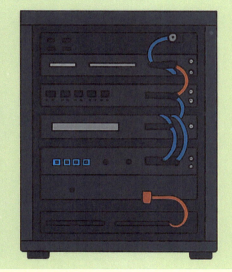

Line Drawings diagram showcasing signal flow in presentation room

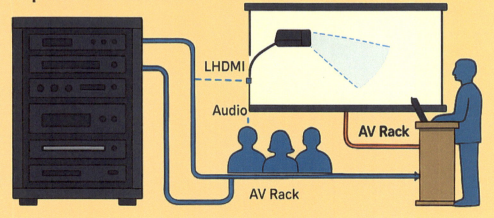

Chapter 6
Floor Plans & AV System Integration

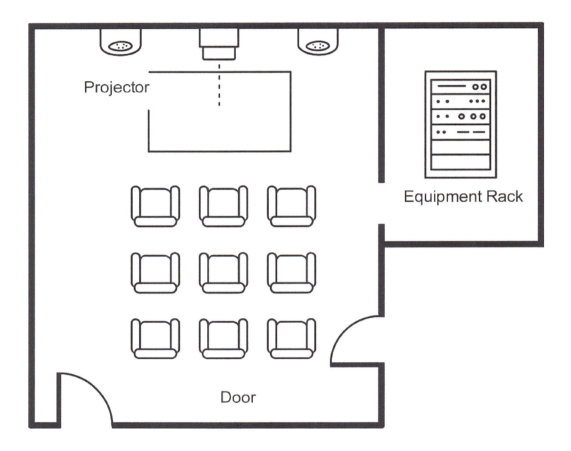

Chapter 6
Floor Plans & AV System Integration

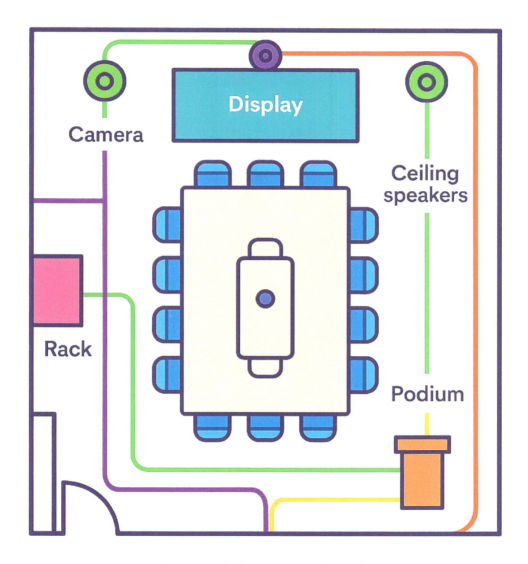

Routing cabling paths for optimal signal distribution

CHAPTER 7
AutoCAD Annotations & Documentation

Adding callouts and dimensions in an AV layout

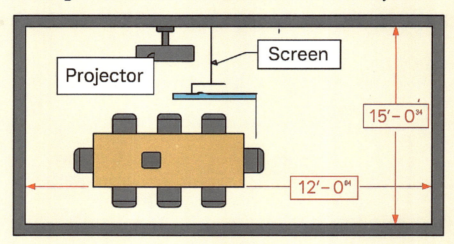

Example of an annotated AV system diagram

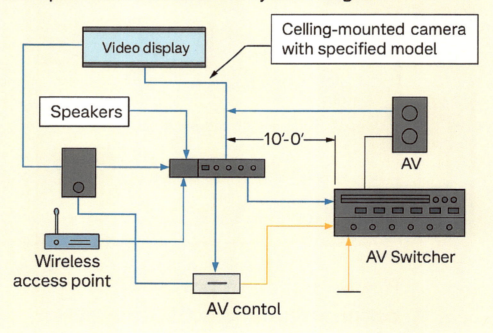

Chapter 7
AutoCAD Annotations & Documentation

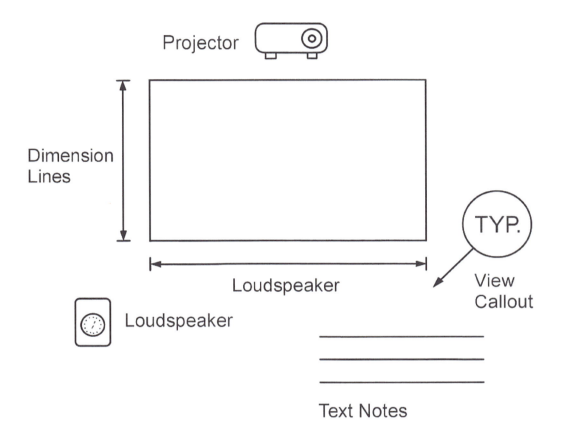

Chapter 8
Future Trends in AV System Design

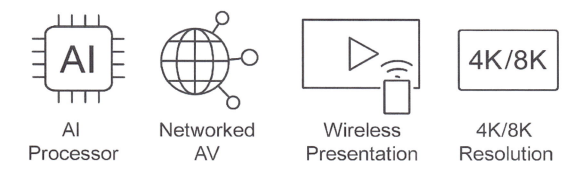

| AI Processor | Networked AV | Wireless Presentation | 4K/8K Resolution |

Chapter 9
Display & Touch Panel Elevations in AV Design

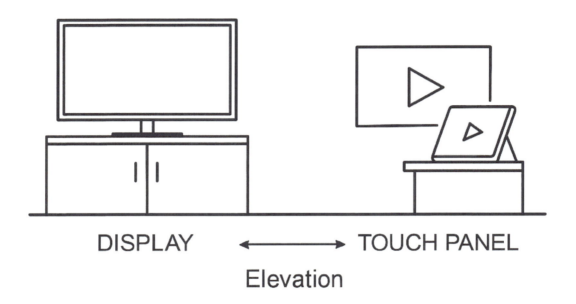

DISPLAY ⟷ TOUCH PANEL

Elevation

Chapter 9
Display & Touch Panel Elevations in AV Design

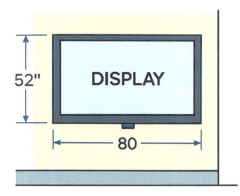

Elevation drawing of
a wall-mounted display

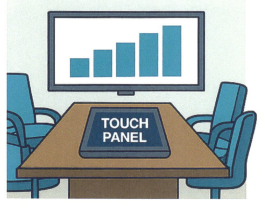

Touch panel integration
in a boardroom setup

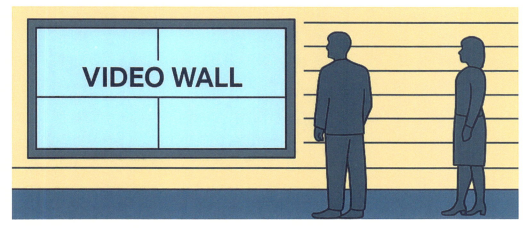

Elevation view of a video wall in
a corporate setting

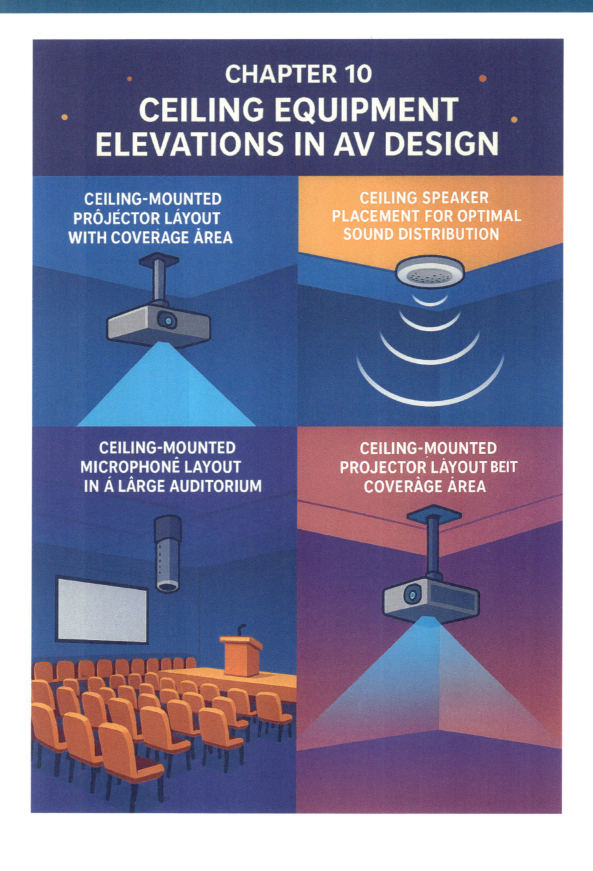

Chapter 11: Essential AV Standards & AUCADC Resources

AV STANDARDS

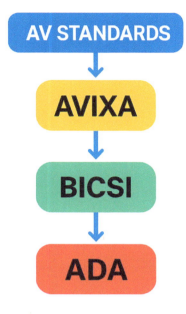

AVIXA

BICSI

ADA

Resour Links

- cadresources.com
- avsymbols.org

Key Standards

COMPLIANCE

Standard	Description
ANSI	Safety standards
ISO	International standards
NFPA	Fire protection
IBC	Building codes
FCC	Communications

Chapter 12: Advanced AV CAD Techniques & Automation

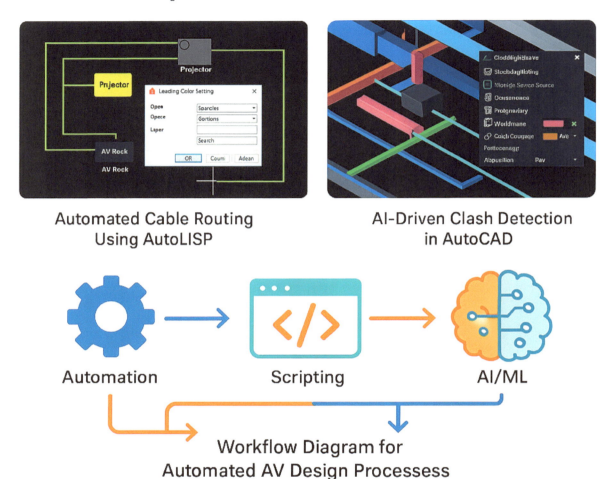

Automated Cable Routing
Using AutoLISP

AI-Driven Clash Detection
in AutoCAD

Automation   Scripting   AI/ML

Workflow Diagram for
Automated AV Design Processess

CHAPTER 12

Advanced AV CAD Techniques & Automation

Automation and advanced CAD techniques can significantly streemeline AV system design. This chapter covers script-based automation for generating drawings, efficiency tips and tools, and the use of parametric modeling to optimize AV design.

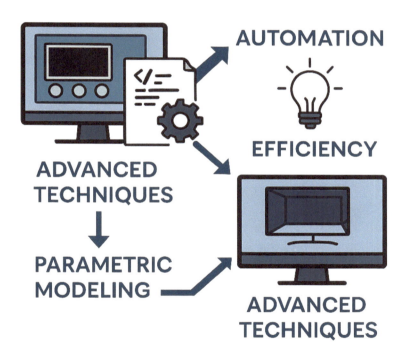

AUTOMATION

EFFICIENCY

ADVANCED TECHNIQUES

PARAMETRIC MODELING

ADVANCED TECHNIQUES

Chapter 13: AutoCAD Troubleshooting & Optimization

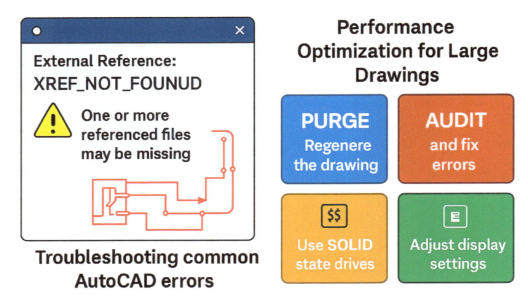

External Reference: XREF_NOT_FOUNUD

⚠️ One or more referenced files may be missing

Troubleshooting common AutoCAD errors

Performance Optimization for Large Drawings

PURGE Regenere the drawing

AUDIT and fix errors

💲 Use **SOLID** state drives

Ε Adjust display settings

AutoCAD Troubleshooting Steps

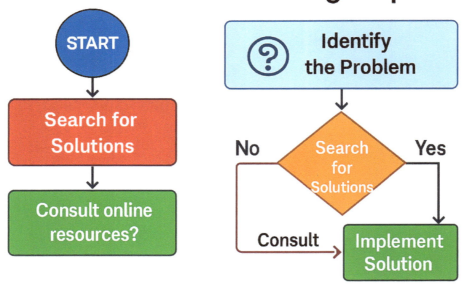

START

Search for Solutions

Consult online resources?

Identify the Problem

No — Search for Solutions — Yes

Consult → Implement Solution

CHAPTER 13

AutoCAD Troubleshooting & Optimization

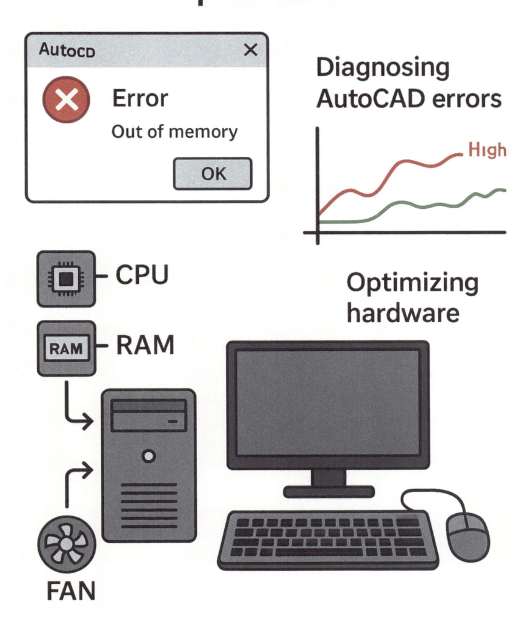

Diagnosing AutoCAD errors

Optimizing hardware

CHAPTER 13

AutoCAD Troubleshooting & Optimization

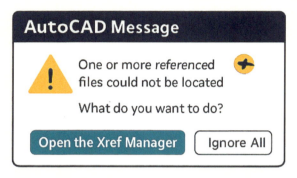

AutoCAD Message

⚠️ One or more referenced files could not be located

What do you want to do?

[Open the Xref Manager] [Ignore All]

- **Disable Hardware Acceleration**
- **Purge Unused Objects**

Flowchart of common AutoCAD troubleshooting steps

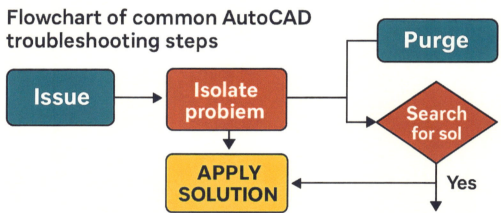

Issue → **Isolate problem** → **Purge**

Isolate problem → **APPLY SOLUTION**

Search for sol → Yes

APPLY SOLUTION ← **Search for sol**

Performance optimization techniques for large drawings

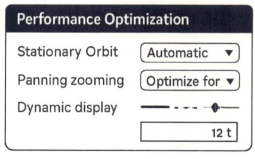

Performance Optimization

Stationary Orbit	Automatic ▼
Panning zooming	Optimize for ▼
Dynamic display	—•— - •—•🔘
	12 t

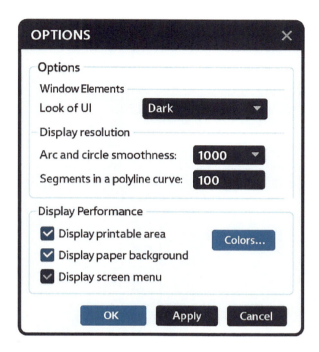

OPTIONS ✕

Options

Window Elements

Look of UI   Dark ▼

Display resolution

Arc and circle smoothness: 1000 ▼

Segments in a polyline curve: 100

Display Performance

☑ Display printable area   [Colors...]

☑ Display paper background

☑ Display screen menu

[OK]   [Apply]   [Cancel]

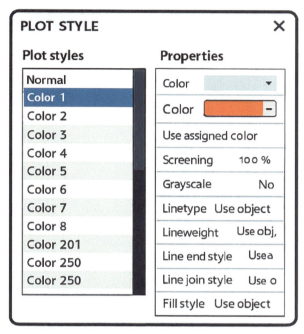

PLOT STYLE ✕

Plot styles   **Properties**

Normal	Color ▼
Color 1	Color ▬
Color 2	Use assigned color
Color 3	
Color 4	Screening 100 %
Color 5	
Color 6	Grayscale No
Color 7	Linetype Use object
Color 8	Lineweight Use obj,
Color 201	Line end style Usea
Color 250	Line join style Use o
Color 250	Fill style Use object

TROUBLESHOOTING CHECKLIST

☐ Signal dropouts

☐ Audio feedback

☐ Video alignment

☐ Control system failures

☐ Network connectivity

☐ Equipment overheating

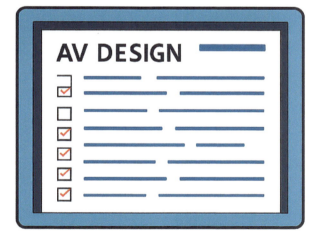

AV DESIGN

APPENDIX

AUTOCAD SETTINGS AND TROUBLESHOOTING

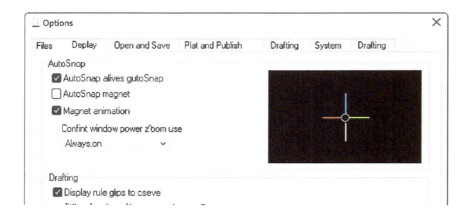

Common Issues and Solutions

 Improve performance by adjusting graphics settings and using hardware acceleration.

 Reset AutoCAD settings or update the software to resolve crashes

 Switch between Graphics Window settings (e.g. Windows, DirectX 11) to fix display issu.

Workflow and Best Practices

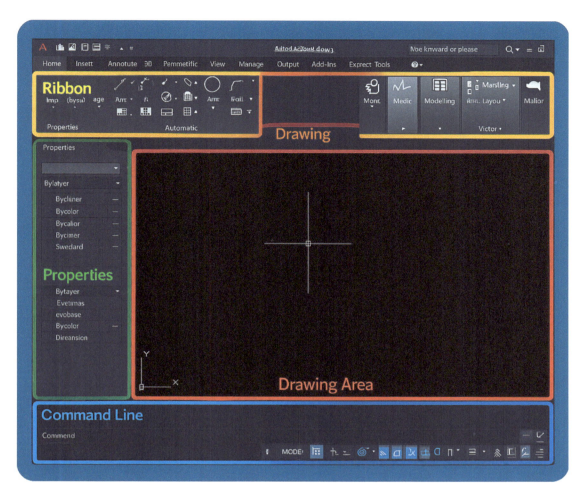

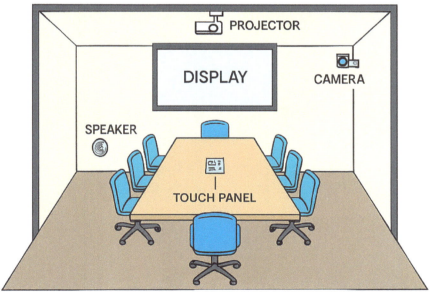

About the Author: Francine Hawkins-Alegeh

A Leader in AV, Construction, and Project Management

Francine Hawkins-Alegeh is a seasoned Entrepreneur, AV Design Engineer, CAD Specialist, Fire Alarm Designer, Intercom Designer and Project Manager with over 24 years of experience in AV system design, construction, and consulting. She has worked on complex AV system integrations for higher education, corporate environments, government buildings, and smart home projects.

Expertise & Specializations

✓ **AV System Design & Integration** – Creating signal flow diagrams, equipment layouts, and technical schematics.
✓ **AutoCAD & Revit** – Leveraging cutting-edge CAD tools for precision engineering and design.
✓ **Project Management** – Leading large-scale AV and construction projects with strategic planning and execution.
✓ **Construction & Real Estate Studies** – Expanding knowledge in construction management, contracts, and real estate licensing.

Francine has also earned multiple industry certifications to expand her expertise in AV design, construction, and business operations.

Professional Experience

Francine has held key roles in various industries, contributing to highly technical and large-scale projects:

◆ **Higher Education Installations** – Designed AV systems for institutions like:
  ☐ University of Alabama at Birmingham (UAB)
  ☐ Florida Gulf Coast University

◆ **Corporate and Government Projects** – Led installations and designs for boardrooms, conference spaces, and corporate technology systems.

  ☐ Jackson, MS Courthouse

◆ **AV Integration and Construction Projects** – Worked on large-scale commercial installations, including video walls, digital signage, and advanced AV solutions.

Education & Certifications

Francine holds multiple degrees and certifications that demonstrate her expertise in technology management, construction, and real estate.

🎓 **Master of Science in Technology Management** – Texas A&M University-Commerce (4.0 GPA)
🎓 **Bachelor of Applied Arts and Science** – Graduated Magna Cum Laude (3.83 GPA)
🎓 **Construction Management Studies** – Focusing on Contracts and Risk Management
🎓 **Real Estate Studies** – Completed coursework and preparing for final licensing exams

Certifications and Licenses:

✔ **Certified Associate in Project Management (CAPM)**
✔ **Certified Technology Specialist (CTS)**
✔ **Certified Systems Design Engineer**
✔ **Six Sigma Green and Yellow Belt**
✔ **Certified Custodial Technician**
✔ **Certified Drone Operator**
✔ **Licensed Texas All Lines Insurance Adjuster**
✔ **Certified Professional Food Manager**
✔ **Certified Notary Signing Agent & Texas Notary Public**

Entrepreneurship & Business Ventures

Francine is the founder and owner of multiple successful businesses in AV design, consulting, construction, and financial services:

◆ **Alegeh Drafting and Consulting Services** – Specializing in AV system design, drafting, and consulting.
◆ **F.D. Hawkins Painting and Remodeling** – A full-service painting and remodeling company handling residential projects.
◆ **Five Dimension Group** – Providing project management, consulting, and drafting solutions.

◆ **Alegeh Notary Services** – Offering notary and loan signing services across Texas.

◆ **Alegeh Insurance & Financial Services** – Specializing in All Lines insurance adjusting, financial literacy, and risk assessment.
◆ **Mobile Alcohol & Beverage Services** – A pop-up bar and beverage catering company serving unique alcohol experiences.

Author & Educator

Beyond her technical and business expertise, Francine is also a published author, online educator, and mentor. She has written three books and is currently developing:

▣ **An Audiobook on AV and System Design** – Covering installation, system integration, permits, codes, and contracts.
▣ **A Self-Paced Advanced AV CAD Course** – Teaching AutoCAD, AV system flow, and construction documentation.

Podcast & Media Work

☐ **"Francine The Butterbean" Podcast** – Focused on tech, travel, culture, and business, with an emphasis on how African Americans can leverage these industries.

☐ **"Unbreakable: Your Story Isn't Over"** – A podcast and Facebook platform dedicated to supporting survivors of abuse, bullying, and suicidal thoughts.

A Visionary in AV & Construction

Francine Hawkins-Alegeh is passionate about empowering professionals in AV, construction, and engineering. Through her teaching, consulting, and business ventures, she continues to bridge the gap between technology, education, and real-world application.